OUTLANDISH

Jo Clement was born in Darlington in 1986. She received a Northern Writers' Award in 2012. She is Editor of *Butcher's Dog* poetry magazine, and founded the imprint Wagtail with support from the European Roma Institute for Arts and Culture (ERIAC). *Butcher's Dog* published her anthology *Wagtail: The Roma Women's Poetry Anthology* in 2021. Her poems have been shortlisted for the Bridport, Melita Hume and Troubadour International prizes. She has written for *The Travellers' Times*, RomaTrial and BBC Radio 4, where she has also been a guest on *Poetry Please*. She was awarded an inaugural AHRC Northern Bridge scholarship for her PhD in Creative Writing from Newcastle University. She is a Creative Writing Lecturer at Northumbria University, and lives in North Shields.

Her first book-length collection, *Outlandish*, was published by Bloodaxe Books in 2022, drawing on new work as well as poems from her debut pamphlet *Moveable Type* (New Writing North, 2020), and from a collaborative walking and writing book, also titled *Outlandish*, co-authored with Damian Le Bas with drawings by W. John Hewitt, which was commissioned by New Writing North for the 2019 Durham Book Festival.

JO CLEMENT

OUTLANDISH

BLOODAXE BOOKS

First published 2022 by
Bloodaxe Books Ltd,
Eastburn,
South Park,
Hexham,
Northumberland NE46 1BS

www.bloodaxebooks.com
For further information about Bloodaxe titles
please visit our website and join our mailing list
or write to the above address for a catalogue.

Supported using public funding by
**ARTS COUNCIL
ENGLAND**

Cover design: Neil Astley & Pamela Robertson-Pearce.

Printed in Great Britain by Bell & Bain Limited, Glasgow, Scotland, on
acid-free paper sourced from mills with FSC chain of custody certification.

You'd better get born in someplace else.
Move along, get along,
Move along, get along.
Go. Move. Shift!

ACKNOWLEDGEMENTS

In 2012 my poems were selected by Paul Farley for a Northern Writers' Award from New Writing North. This supported my writing at a vital time.

With many thanks I acknowledge the inaugural Northern Bridge scholarship awarded to me by the Arts and Humanities Research Council. Without such faith and generous funding, I could not have written this book. Thanks to further support from the School of English at Newcastle University. I travelled to Connecticut to debut my poems and research collections at the Beinecke Library and Yale Center for British Art. I am very grateful to my supervisor Professor Sean O'Brien for hearing the music: thank you. Special thanks must also go to Dr Pippa Little and Dr Christy Ducker for reading with full hearts. This is for my family.

Some of these poems were included in *Outlandish,* a collaborative walking and writing book co-authored with Damian Le Bas with drawings by W. John Hewitt commissioned by New Writing North for the 2019 Durham Book Festival with Arts Council England support, and in my pamphlet *Moveable Type* (New Writing North, 2020).

CONTENTS

PREFATORY NOTE

'Memory,' writes John Berger, 'works radially,' In *About Looking* (1980), he illustrates this idea with eight black lines in a sunbeam pattern: a flash, the kind of persistent spectre of floating light we might squint away in a curtained passport booth. Photographs serve as *aide-mémoire* to their viewer or unzip a portal to a more unfamiliar past.

I wrote the poems in *Outlandish* to pay deep attention to an archive of *in media res* images that pre-date photography: wood engravings by the Northumberland-born printmaker Thomas Bewick. The four miniature illustrations in this book are reproductions of his tail-pieces, visual markers that conclude or bridge textual passages in the ornithological field guide *A History of British Birds* (1797). A selection of these outlying vignettes delineates the peripherality of Gypsy, Roma and Traveller peoples in the Western imagination, whereas others speak to my writing practice.

In the first tail-piece, a leaf blows from the impenetrable hawthorn copses that fenced-off privatised common land in the long eighteenth century. Enclosure shifted Travellers into peripheral spaces, exposing our tents and wheeled homes to more than just the elements. For centuries, Travellers have lived in poverty and, following the pastoral rhythms of seasonal labour, would disappear from one town to appear on the edges of another. These peripatetics are fuelled by embodied memories of capital punishment and diaspora. The current Police, Crime, Sentencing and Courts Bill is pressing to make peripatetic living illegal, part of seemingly endless iterations of our presence in Britain being unpicked, as Wordsworth described it, like a knot.

The contested space of Traveller identity manifests in the second engraving. Impressed upon a windowpane, a fingerprint disrupts our view of distant farmland to the right, and from the left, we half-spy a horse and its rider. The vignette appears to record a momentary, inadvertent touch on glass. Yet, we do not know to whom these human oils belong. Are we, the viewer, indoors and in touching distance of the open air beyond? Or, is the print on the outside of the glass made by someone looking *in*? This threshold space signifies the continuing struggle of Travellers as feared outsiders, wishing to be understood as an ethnic group whose identity is not bound to a particular way of life but whose survival once depended upon it.

My poems leap towards and vault away from these artworks, as well as the birds they accompany in the original natural history guide. They are ekphrases of a kind, as illustrated by the third tail-piece. Art is represented by a daubed palette with brushes, music by a tightly-strung lyre and poetry, by a plush wreath, representing those ancient Greek laurels placed upon the heads of poets. Correspondence between the disciplines of visual, literary and sonic expression is integral to my writing. For this viewer, Bewick's tail-pieces made Traveller people and places more proximate, but as demonstrated in the fourth illustration, these renderings were not always favourable. This soft-edged vignette presents a fixed viewpoint of six Travellers gathered around a fire. The engraving technique selected for his subjects is the cruder black line, rather than his preferred white 'fine line' technique which contributed to his major innovations to the printed book. We can infer that the group are Travellers because we can see the prominent cartwheel, the dharmachakra that today features on the Gypsy, Roma and Traveller flag. Though a people of no official place, there we are, nestled in Northern English woodlands. The horse is elsewhere. In the hand of the central figure is a woven basket – also known as a *trushnie* – used for foraging and hawking. Here, it has been used as a creel, to carry a fish, presented to the family as supper. Such a basket could also carry wild-picked flowers, to make selling on foot in steady market towns easier, a tradition that still holds.

On the cover of this collection is a photograph of the internationally-acclaimed Outsider artist Delaine Le Bas taken by Tim Walker in 1998. For at least four generations, amongst other occupations such as car-breaking and roofing, her Traveller family were flower sellers. In place of the handbag with its lucky black and white sequined cat, we might well imagine a willow trushnie full of softest gypsophila and tight-lipped daffodils, arranged from their heads to the tips of cut stalks. Le Bas, too, has been arranged. She steps out from a verdant Bewick hedge and brings us into the Oz-like now. Disembodied, Le Bas' shoes reflect the sky, reminding us in L. Frank Baum's novel, the Wicked Witch of the East wears silver, not ruby slippers. Her neat Vyshyvankan-style embroidered skirt is visibly pinned to the gnarly thicket. This is an image of contradiction, in which the skirt appears both flat-ironed and also billowy as if the otherwise still figure were spinning. Le Bas' subject matters too, are caught between one-dimensional representations of identity and lived Traveller experiences, notably her performances as the 'Untouchable Gypsy Witch' and 'The Romani Embassy'. As with the poems in *Outlandish*, Le Bas utilises cultural memory radially, drawing from the past and the present to confront and challenge damaging perceptions, whilst holding space to embrace those cultural traditions and practices that serve to make us who we are.

The Impression of Water

You know which way the wind is blowing
in a Bewick, if it blows at all or blows
a gale. How fast the water flows in lines

against the Traveller's face, her clothes,
the supplementary weight. Dampen paper
to print still water and the impression

of water from sky. It starts backwards,
on reflection. Follow the swan's example
when writing on a page of river: glide.

Family Silver

Let me sing of my greatest
grandfather's knife. He graved

the tooth with scrimshaw cobs,
so he might remember to handle

the blade as gently as his horses.
Kept it sharp enough to gut a trout,

split a clutch of pegs. Sharper
still to cross palms with silver,

he called it *churi*, sweet-talked maids
between their lady's petticoats.

How strange those fingers
might squeeze a noble waist.

Left on the grass,
an open wooden hand.

churi: a multi-purpose knife used to make pegs.

Vault

Housed away, she waits on him.
Picks anagylpta petals,

lifts carpet to watch
silverfish dance,

thrive on nowt
but damp and dirt

and as a polecat slips
between t-shirt

and torso, the metal blind
snaps shut.

Outside, Lascelles,
where milk's skimmed

and little girls
get dragged up

in hand-me-downers,
flat upon flat

occupied by darkness.
Where roaches are spent

scratchcards, mad cows fall
in heat or tip loose

from public houses.
She'll chalk a fence

Lascaux.
Leggy horses lost

to a corrugate
flash of rain,

as the hooves pull in
at Honeypot Lane.

II

There's a rifle in the cupboard
and the dogs need walked.

Back and forth a ball drums
the house wall, edging the urn

they can't agree what to do with,
forward. The girls ride

leaning gravestones
like ponies,

their mouths stuck
with brambling,

nettle-stung ankles
grazed giddiup green.

They smash bees
from jam jars, run,

as the lads kick the ball
against the wall

where he's sleeping,
till his fists scream

on the glass
and they flush out

like so many bees
or game, back to the Moor,

where porn pulps open crotches
on lamp-posts which blush

and blink as the buses come in
asking for exact change

and leave without passengers
or windows.

III

Weather walks toward the house,
or her grandfather,

smart as a peg in his old straw hat
and breezing with the fallen May.

The street saw him coming,
biggest bloke in the steel mill

his gold rings hooking sunlight
as he hands a cane by the crook.

This is a branch to truss a tent on,
or curve a beck from bank to bank.

His sloe arm moves her still,
lifts till vaulting, she stamps the air.

Inheritance

His sovereign rings splay my fingers
                like we're holding hands again.

Back then I'd press them on my skin
                until they etched bloodless glyphs

in my palms, signet circles, Saints.
                Revenant horseheads

bare the same teeth I cut mine on, those
                diamonds, diamonds, diamonds.

'King Faa' (opposite page): *patrìn:* grass used as a communicative marker of passage; *bow-top:* the stretched green canvas roof on a Traveller's wagon; *coney:* rabbit.

King Faa

No patrìn, no shock
of grass, his moonlit flit

brings farness. No kettleflute
till Christmas,

no fiddlescrape,
or bow-top brake.

Trunk by trunk
embowers her,

where he blackened tea
and whittled fingers,

tin pinched tight
as coney skin.

She wills the wood
to darken,

urges a nightjar to chirr
his haggle's shape,

let horse dealer hands
take wing in soft claps

that swoop and slap
themselves away.

Elsewhere he drops
a flight feather;

her heartwood hears it fall.
She picks up the tracks

of the green man who passes
from this wood, to that.

Teesdale Erratics

Overnight they arrive in the gap
between the prefabs,

whose sides are dashed
with pebbles and a sign swung

on one screw:
NO BALL GAMES.

Three boulders are planted
on the grassy path.

Earless skulls
crowned in whitewash,

two-ton, like the chip
the teacher pointed out

on her shoulder. Sent her off
with a slap to the Head.

She comes here instead
to fizz open pop

as she sits on the middle one,
listening for his quad's buzz

up and down
the Queen's highway,

the rider shirtless and at speed
without licence or helmet.

Big Fat Gypsy Swindle

Before he knew they took a twenty
for a tenner, he's back with a dozen eggs

and a kiss, to share her floured cheek.
Soon he'll tap pockets, rile his wallet

and whine *the bastards gypped me*.
How often change falls short,

words cut to the quick, skin her
like an eel but she lets nothing

of the strain slip, except eternity
from a ring finger, to unbutton eggs:

a skein of bloodshot yolks
landing in sifted sugar.

She revs her Gypsy mother's mixer.
Blushes the Christening icing pink.

Cobsong

Untethered from our travel,
                 our tasselled cushions,

this tinker's tongue
                 I should not speak or write.

This horseshoe is a home
                 to hoof the earth

from stopping-place
                 to stopping-place,

pulling cargo in between.
                 What keeps me now

from horses, paper houses?
                 Once I was a foal

dealt at Appleby, river warm,
                 clean as Gypsy linen.

The horse they built a hearse for,
                 buried lake-deep,

marked with stone. Won't you let
          a little air in? Just a breath

handled by the trees
          the breeze that bore the crow.

Or let a fiddle sing our name.
          They say like muddy shoes

it will carry but see how we press
          these petals, seeding as we pass.

The stamp of horses
          broken at night.

At Eildon

Hard into heels, we found ourselves
walking to rise with the Sisters,

the van ever below, safe as houses.
Trusted with distance, you steady the pack

cinching my collar, that pulled me back.
Steep, the old way knew what lived in there,

pressing as a lurcher kneels onto a hare,
brindles its curve into the snow's unrest.

It saw the clearing in a black wood
and a lass behind the lamp,

who looks as I did then, heather-scuffed,
overstepping fizzy wires,

slicing light onto birch backs,
her boots, steel signs. Eildon knows our stake,

Hawkers, Moonmen, Gypsies,
names we tried to hide. Out of Scott's view,

we sit a spell in the saddle
to unshoulder its writhe.

Every stitch read *Trespass*,
I couldn't leave it behind.

Smithsong

Venus thumbs her Bible's gilded fore edge
as her women feel the places

my granda kicks. Pilgrims to her living wagon
pat Lourdes water on pulses, Catholic

Chanel whose sweetness only they can smell.
Alone, she turns to the Song of Songs

to sing him still. Between cedar beams
she sings his hart neck, the chains of gold

her baby will wear at nineteen, his company
of horses, apples and figs. Later, he pours tea

and sings her fair, her Lebanon smell,
the secret places of the stairs. She counts

the bubbles for luck then shuts the book,
holds their place in the song with a tarot card.

Market

Down the road, Traveller girls
wear fur-free bombers,

all tiger stripes, organic cotton.
But they don't care

about Stella McCartney's
commitment to sustainability,

they've got free ice creams
and pups. Elsewhere,

there was a press release:
back to school with the Big Top,

ringmasters, animated print.
The photographer says

turn a cartwheel, girls
but they shy away

pinch petunias
from pub planters,

push stalks behind ears.
None of these bairns

is called Tilly
or Lillian, the names

of their free coats
and they don't need to be told

to act tough like the kids
who make the billboard.

Mass

No communion in County Clare,
no laying on of hands.

Father turfs out the women
for not dressing right. Locks up,

strikes a rollie. Rings the Guard.
He'll *not give mass to gobshites*.

Back and forth and laced in ribbon
the babby shakes his rattle,

peers out from his Silver Cross.
She knows he'll not settle.

The Sly and Unseen Day

Blind-eyes. Untapped estates.
A sinkful of cracked light.

Freight-flicker, something far
brought near. Hoss-first

he smelts the panes, bugles:
oooanyragandbone?

By now it's rhetorical.
Streets pretend not to hear.

From marrow to metal,
tatters turned to lift hardware,

strip white goods not rags.
Today she carts a Yugo.

Strimmer on the backseat,
hoover beside.

Her scrape slows traffic,
horns trailing behind

and in this edge-made-centre,
Hazel's sat up on the roof,

one hand to steady reins,
the other winds up the copper.

Yugo: a Yugoslavian car produced during the 1970s.

Tinker's Tea

The Settle line brought me to these hills.
Maned with winter, he makes tea the old way
and I thank stars for the lack of a service desk,
pylons or ticket checks. Behind the private road,

I put a leaf back in my book, to watch blue shadows
hawk the snow. He tells me my hair has grown,
asks how my studies go, pours the best hot air
from spout to mouth. Her recipe breathes spice.

The right berries steeped with cloveroot, woodruff
and hogweed: it's no secret I came for the leaves
in this pot. But the real gift was seeing
him for the first time in a coat.

Knots

Blushed with blood and false summits, outcast,
        I keep a familiar distance. Without wind cheats

or the right shoes, I have words with mountains.
        Accent bending in the wind, I eke aloud

Wordsworth's *Gipsies*, the lines hung over me
        hawk-like, as his cloud-double slips the Screes

toward Appleby. Our luck lands blackly there too.
        He saw us as spots, a spectacle, knots.

The same fight picked in private fields.
        Is it time to move on? Let me sit this stone

on the marker's pile. Tell the capital I am a Traveller
        under open sky and yes, our bonfire's still raging.

Screes: a fell in the Lake District between Patterdale and Ambleside.

Larch

Uprooted from Carpathian crests, we burnish
in the *native* green. Out of season,

he mistrusts our sudden height
but can't convince the canopy,

this company of outskirt trees
– each conceding dirt or light to the other –

he finds our fires as foreign as his 'Gipsies'
sheltered here, blanketed by walls

to raise ringlets, *wreaths of smoke*
given back to the silver sky

that shakes with murmurations
of winged pollen, far thunder.

He begged us stop
sporing spectres, burnt Beltane boughs

to ward us off returning
to the near-dark. Listen low enough

you'll hear us trailing needled shawls
down the Corpse Road, larch sisters

bewitching the fell's even black
with a bloomery of cast-iron tongues.

Our feet forge ember passage,
keep on *overrunning these hills.*

The Graver

Digging in the dark
I scuff shoulders,
unearth a stirrup
from the Steppe,

moored so long ago
it turned lyre string, sang
who are these coming
to the sacrifice?

Ladies Day fox furs
and fascinators,
screwed-up slips.
Greed as long

in the tooth
as grave goods
or steeple-high
hawthorn. A gamble

on bones bred
so light they shatter.
Step out of tack,
Whistlejacket,

leave those airs
above ground.
No horse should
be buried at a canter.

Wild Camp

To hell with the abbey,
we found a place between the pebbles —

> *look, a heron by the edges, peripheral*
> *flies over —*

so here we are, bivvied by the Tweed like two rocks
and yeah, I suppose the patriarchy won't have fucked off

until we can stop talking about *man hours, stag dos*
and my pay matches yours —

> *see the angler making his way down?*
> *he's rivered to his thighs,*
> *a shadow casting out lines into the darkness,*
> *the fish jumping for flies —*

or perhaps it's when we no longer need to explain
how two people might walk, talk and sleep together

like this without any such complication

or even write
a poem without a Gypsy in it, oh no it's too late —

> *listen, the birds are dying off —*

Ironwork, V&A

There's not a pot to piss in. Least not the kind I'm looking for.
Move on, she said. *You read too much into these things.*

Still, our kettles boil, crucibles stew and sing. Their withy hooks
turn to litterfall. Wooden limbs left behind, long eaten.

But the iron pots we wrought, have they not weathered here
or found their place amongst the crested railings, locked gates

and all their keys? Now I see them loosed from wall and earth,
were these black balustrades not cast by the fiery Smiths?

withy hook: a camp kitchen made from branches such as willow.

Outlandish

Conied in scraps, her Meg is cast,
        creeks oak-slow and ashen

hoyed men at floodlights
        lifting the hot glare of lint.

This seer, this Sibyl, burst flax to flames,
        tore her voice to rags. The papers

coined her a foreign familiar:
        the *Gypsiness* of weird women,

pythons, queens. Tell us, Cushman,
        how the curtain skimmed your ankle,

sounding that inner applause
        that you can take off the dress.

hoy: toss, hurl (Northumbrian).

Haunt

Something about not wanting
to be touched

kept us coming back.
Or the smell.

I'm galloping away on it, now.
You caught me first

by the beach. Lids tight,
lungs full of hoss,

nodding to the hooves'
dropped rhythm.

I couldn't tell you
we were Gypsies,

admit to the skim
of blood that can't settle,

that the landscape
I am in has to change.

You'd never take in
the air at Appleby Fair,

so thick with horse
and home. Shirtless kids

riding bareback
in the rain

and the sound
of wet hoof on wet stone.

Crown

These are the standing stones,
and what feet they have known,

to crown Yetholm's Kings
and Queens. No plaque marks

the place, they define themselves
keeping oaths given to the wind,

smoked peat-blue as turf
that knew no border. Off and on,

they'd take your ears
for using the wrong tongue,

so we held them dear
as bairns to the breast,

sharp as ground knives.
At Stob Stane, Spey has me

by the throat, as I step up
to hear the Common.

Paisley

With India's hand on the loom,
I untwist a paisley square

from round my neck:
red, green and gold

threads repeat almonds
some call figs, figs the Welsh

call pears and pears you might
call teardrops. Shook onto

the grass, I smooth out Kashmir
— so close to silk —

over the fault line made
of my body: feet in England,

head in Scotland,
a heart elsewhere.

Vardo

rut thud the rim

BASIL BUNTING

Sure as the colts
will nag the fillies
our living wagon

prints itself
across my mind.
Lacquered

like spring woods
where it 'atches
a spell,

it's all cut
in bonny birds
and brushed

with roses,
windows laced
with cockled glass.

A wheel-bird
sent up
from its scrape

turns like silver
in pockets or my head
in this flat,

tight as bow-top tarp
static as pike
skin on flame.

vardo: a horse-drawn Traveller's wagon with a stretched green canvas roof, also called a 'living wagon'; *'atch:* to make camp.

A Stopping-place

That year he pulled up to pick fruit they were waiting
in the trees. He'd never seen the like. Apples,

endless apples. A summer's cider laid to waste,
spoils under high sun. First branches tottered chew-

chew-chew then down an unfamiliar flock flew,
to shear russet flesh with twisted bills. Not eating a scrap

except shiny seeds. Hawk-armed, he threw himself
into a scarecrow. Their shadows exited the field.

No stoppage that year. No market. No fair.
A swarming of pitchforks and bees.

Craft

Soon, like the first oar carved in oak, our tents called
for wheels. Horse-pulled vardos spun

on necessity's nave, Rom found harbour under bow-top
eaves tight nocked and steeped in mordant green. Lessons

in light opened windows, knives released roosting wagtails
from cedar, split the lips of boxing hares. These wains

hooped with leaves of gilt, generations stood proud
in the shiving light they were built by,

votives for the Golden Rule that we should only do
as we'd be done to. Wagon time passes by like smoke.

Rom: a Traveller of Romani origin; *wagon time:* the life span of a horse-drawn
Traveller's wagon.

Pome

back then you'd hang
for a skirtful of windfall

gypsy would nail an ear
to a trunk or a palm

red as ribbons
wounding

May

.

your childhood apples
were tarred in toffee

mirror-sharp let to rust
on table tops once bitten

i only ever chew
through the core

with little care
for your watching

or the seed's bright poison
it was then I told you

about the orchard
twig between my teeth

.

see if I draw this apple
round my hip bone

you've drawn it too
on your cheek

Pollard

Starlings pick at pink gristle
as we sit under the canopy.

A chapter he says,
arms getting heavy

with apples. Against the wind,
the prop sways all our hips

and shoulders touched
by the branch-shadow's

blackness. He marks the collars,
winter points to prune.

We mustn't stress the limbs.
Pollarded eyes regard him,

her freckled hands
in the window lifting nets

to arrange polished porcelain
to say we are horse people.

We've settled.

Playing Cards

Granda Jack plays patience in his new flat,
his heart fixed on Kings, on returning

the deck to their suits: first ace cards, numbers,
then court. Across the ledge his carved elephants

parade trunk-to-tail, backlit by an Indian summer
brewing pink. Their meaning was lost on me, then,

like the door, always propped open by the pot plant
we bought to celebrate his moving in.

This game soon has him beat. He jumbles cards
back together, soughs. We go to the park,

key open sardines, headless silver flounders
in our oily fingers as we pinch them out.

This is the life, he says, pulling bones through his teeth.
I didn't know I was born until he told me

what it meant to call a spade a spade or a Traveller
a pike. How a boy my age hid from the Reich,

bound hooves in hessian and hay to flit town
in the dead of night, wraithing cobbles to keep quiet

our bad blood. Or how we moved into white woods,
burnt fiddles to warm ribs, sang low in the slack tents

their boots stamped and upturned. Black triangles
needled to our chests like stars, badges of shame

that marked us work-shy *Zigeuner*.
The death camps devoured us. Tonight,

the shapes that keep me from sleep are square
and on paper, the kind I falter over:

Ethnic Origin, Please Tick One:
White □ or Gypsy □

Zigeuner: the German noun to describe 'asocial' Travellers.

Self-portrait as 100 Travellers

Here. No good. Nomad. Roma. Rover.
Rom. Dom. Rai. Raider. Reiver.
Truant. Turnpike. Trash. Tatter.
Tinner. Tinker. Toad. Trickster.
Tinsmith. Tar-macker. Boater. Tea
leaf. Pedlar. Potter. King. Cuckoo.
Knot. Outlaw. Trespasser. Straw hat.
Scrapper. Johnny. Faa. Moone-man.
Fly. Fitter. Flitter. Migrant. Sharper.
Harper. Dipper. Sleeper. Soothsayer.
Heathcliff. Hawker. Knacker. Clogger.
Lock. Idler. Thief. Jailbird. Lovell.
Boswell. Lee. Waggon-carried.
Wayfarer. Crooked. Filthy. Floater.
Vagrant. Vermin. Band. Muse.
Wanderer. Journeyer. Vagabond.
Smith. Gadabout. Me. Flashy. Scum.
Will o'the wisp. Lowlife. Rambler.
Pathfinder. Drifter. Carny. Chav. Dog.
Dregs. Carmen. Maggie. Meg. Dove.
Ratter. Pilgrim. Pedlar. Seer. Witch.
Rabble. Raggle-taggle. Rag-and-bone.
Gitano. Egyptian. Gyprat. Gypsy.
Gipsy. Gyppo. PIKEY. Gone.

Wonderful Fish

A fish in the mouth of a silver swan
is eaten endlessly. Beak closed,

he holds it under his tongue,
until the show of clockwork lets it play.

A fish moth sits under my tongue, too,
born between the pages of a glued

paper house. Such a small fish,
silvered, it lives between my teeth,

swimming in the slaver, tickling
its way to speak of our lost vardo,

the sulky horse. Of silk scarves it might
make holes in, of books it might

make homes in. For the fish who can eat
the binding, can eat *The Bible*.

Giftorse

Fleet of foot, he's of the same black line in my blood,
        the skim that can't settle. There beneath the hedgehog

and the snake, he takes my grandfather's shape, crossing
        a river-like road. Where else could I find him

but fording between Fables? This pressed man steers me back,
        sudden as the tap of sovereigns on glass.

Let him turn his cards again, the Traveller whose kippers
        smoked my skin, the man who carried an apple, from where?

From where he came he brought us brass, a horsehead tacked
        to the wall, to stop the luck from failing keys.

A clutch would find themselves caught on his ear
        like a whistle of song or a pierced gold ring.

Nightjar

behind black there's light

JOHN BERGER

Printer ink costs more per glass
than champagne, so I read poems

off my phone instead. Dad's hands
weren't always on backwards,

they used to dig graves, candle eggs
against summers. When it started

he'd take himself away, come back
worse. Now he's stuck in this bed.

Let me be my father's daughter,
roll tobacco, tell him

how street walks work in Yale,
that men there willed me Irish,

how Beineke marble strained light,
how glad I was of rain.

That day three blue jays
perched on my motel window,

fluted off into the street, sounding
the same rusty rifles I heard

when I followed his poaching.
Tell me again about the nightjar

roosting in her moonlit scrape
the air shaken like a Jew's harp.

Dad's blind in one eye.
We share this way of seeing.

I saw his black-eyed migrant
long before Bewick's.

The Romani Star

They sidestep her wagon like a homeless sleeper,
      steel themselves toward trains or gauge a distance

safe enough to crane necks through the doorway,
      past the painted signs: *Come in,*

let me change your luck. £3. I am a True Rom,
      I have Travelled the World. Angeline pulled in

under the Bigg Market alder. A tree set in concrete,
      however that works. Under its breath,

the street has its own opinions. Once this place spun
      with cartwheels, stacked with creaking wicker,

barley warm as bantams: now a late-licence market
      for a different kind of cattle. She'll be off

before pigeon-chested lads give chase to moonshine,
      hatred or heels. Cash in hand, I step up the stair

into the Star where every surface is an opportunity
      flowered, gilt, cushion or tassel. Catkins dot

the ceiling as we grieve tea leaves black. Outside
      voices fade like the light through the selvedge:

the management reserves the right… I tell her the nuns
      were cruellest to my sister who got the Rom skin

and black eyes. Ash taps into the empty pack. The cane
      kept her from school, too. *But they can't beat*

it out or in, ye see? She turns the cup upside down
      and the finches huddle, rest beaks on their backs.

As she opens out my hands into her palms,
      streetlights wake themselves,

catch the cockle in the pane. A lit peach, the vardo blooms
      as she tells me what's in the lines and leaves.

Le Bûcher

Pine pollen scuds the air
    as they unearth what's left of her.

Offensive to the pious,
    garlanded in May: now a rag,

a rib, a tomcat. Familiar with birds,
    the diviner sang

beside the Ladies' Tree,
    swore on Saints not sprites

and *against all feminine decency*
    gripped a Gospel's hilt.

In Rouen they gave her twice to fire
    where Flaubert saw the smoking

Gypsy camp. Hated, he wrote,
    is *the bedouin, the heretic, the poet.*

Causeway

We're glad of what we're given
and because we must, we walk

between places, our boots shiny
as seal pups. Earlier a crab,

a hot jar of honey. On the island,
I saw swifts flute the ruined chimney,

they'll be in Africa by now.
The sea, always arriving.

Periwinkle

You speak from this edge and colour
the impossible grey, who for once,

holds its breath as you dare to be
so yellow and small, smaller

and more yellow than anything
to ever find this shore. In the eye

of your whorl I see them slipping,
picking cockles at night, fighting

the tide. Not of this sea but that one,
though I don't know how or why

they map a difference. It's all salt.
There is a delicacy and a hardness

to shell, as slight and hollow
as the moment you hear the words

illegal immigrant missing
change to human skull found.

Manes

Come hear the Boer's hooves.
This cavalry canters on, turns

the corner as might a flood
of urgent salmon. Headstrong

they take to tarmac like Tyne,
surfacing not to breed

but to breathe, wearing pocked
sequined skins. This battery

of bodies is a foggy glue-sniff.
Horses who made light of guns,

carried the living, ferried
them home. Nothing but death

could stop these steeds
in their steels. Horseflesh ridden,

shot at, eaten. And yet, not a soul
of them have names here

as men do, in stone. Let me mend
this poor husbandry:

come here filly, tell me your name,
I've a handful of hay.

Polished

I would go to him, the hanging, to keep the company
of his feet. Or watch him sway on windy days,

shadows bruising a parade on the heath. Only clouds
passed there. An illusion of relief, I'd rest his tiptoes

on the Cheviots, my face staring back from the polish,
listen to the hills speak of me and over me,

blowing his coat tails like crow's tails
whose gathering dark vex the arm of wood.

I knew him once, though his hands were not so blue.
Crows carry on coming. Carrion crowing.

Still I stay beneath his soles to hear them
mouth black noise. Beak the fibres of his face.

And one landed on my shoulder to test the softness
of my skin. I started them off, loosened his long laces.

Slid my bare feet in. My hands wore the proof
of their theft. The welt on my cheek burnished with a print.

Travelling Light

Will this be how I learn about travelling light,
cross country with a tent and books on my back?
Is it here, on the walk between hill and river?
Diligence is tiring. By afternoon I'm in an ale house
where I tell him the wealth of my pint is measured
by the thickness of its head and the certainty
of darkness. Proximity's a blessing. In The Crown
and Cushion I forget a button, tell him about the hen
I necked and plucked the summer we couldn't make
ends meet. Her feathers shrouded my feet, my hair
all pinned with down. Necessity, they say, is the mother.
In his family, wealth is measured by the plumpness
of pillows. He pulled a feather from his hat,
closed his hand over mine. *Keep it, cut it to write.*

Rite

At daybreak we crowd the sands between a lacework of baby's-breath
to look at lines of Fairy Liquid, luminous and slick,
drawn along each piebald's spine.

Grease lifts. First withers then river turn to bubbles.
Every year the town is washed of its people.
We're immersed in this baptismal Eden.

Singing Lesson

No free rides here. No summer holiday.
Back when mam couldn't afford tea,
yet alone shoes for our never-ending feet,

        I riled her senseless for a hoss.

That's how he said it. *Hoss*. Light as a skim,
I couldn't shake it, the way I'd seen them
shudder flies.

        I roped her into a lesson.

The lass slapped me in a helmet, clipped me
to the bridle, had me rising up and down,
fairground pink and prim.

She kept saying *Horse. Equestrian.*
Course. Told me to brush my hair
and learn to speak. I only went once.
Cost a tenner.
        When Grandad came back

we took a rag and bone pace
      past the burnt out offie,
no entry signs and pylons.
      Had me up on a muddy cob
slow enough not to spook the traffic,
      down the road where they zipped
sulkies through red lights.

Years apart, my dad and his dad
led this passage, a hand each to his muzzle,
reconciled.
      Steady hoss, this, Son.

The motion steadies me still.
My forebears looking back as my ankles tap out
the hoss's stride. Now the birds murmur his song.

> *She's a bonny lass, can ride 'an hoss*
> *my bairn, our blood, our road.*

The motion steadies me still.

Homecoming

rivered like trout there's this flash lad
on his hoss
spading hooves

his waterway gymkhana
deep as a tall mare

banks hooked on pebbled gaits

as he drowns thunder with heels
cannon bones firing

two fingers up to the council
distant reivers
hair slicked back
no saddle all bridle

then stomach laid to withers
curb chains drape into her mane

as he speaks in private of diving

for a spell

and ear-close they go under
pressed into the anvil black
sunk like a stone

till a bubble breaks
then a hand or an ear

he crests
stood on the mirror of himself
barefoot and dripping

in black-wet denim

      all teeth and chest shining

          half-boy
            half-hoss
              all bray

FLASH!

Out by the fair's edge my shutter's going
like the clappers, to snap these lads

zipping by on sulkies stood in a bevelled blur
of bare chests, hooves and Brylcreem.

Speeds are breakneck in the flashing lane.
No brake, just reins pulled tight

when irons skid on scraps – or gorgers cut
the track – there's knucklebones

and bawling *Oi! Oi! Mind ya backs!*
In rosaries and trackkies, they whip up

dry June heat, immaculate girls beside.
Sat on the bank I take a skeg

through my reel for my best
Sallie Gardner flying in that twenty-

fifth blink when every foot's lifted.
Papers maim it *the mad gypsy mile*

but like first impressions,
you can't trust hooves to the naked eye.

gorger: a non-Traveller; *skeg:* to look.

Prophet Mark

Later on by The Grapes, a shirtless man
led her to his hoss by the thumb,

placed it in a hollow on her neck.
That's a prophet mark there, love.

Feel how it fits? God's thumbprint.
Arab blood. You were meant to ride her.

prophet mark: a dent in musculature that forms around a foal's hoof in utero.

Shoed

Tonight's flung open like a window,
the grass littered with slivers of hoof
the farrier's hand shears loose,
scythes to shoe the passing flock.
Appleby would shoo us, too, if it could.
The locals draw curtains, bolt doors,
shut up shop: take off quick as the keepers
gave my wander onto private grounds
the boot. I'd seen it in the paper:
Wrath of Tipp-Ex Divorcee Who's Down
to her Last Castle, the *Mail* resolved
I'd somehow mind. What a fucking state.
Hollow halls. Curtained walls. Ramparts
a millennium high and we're the feud
you pick? Offshore toffs sold the NHS,
sunk BHS, even tried to sell Blencathra
and there's no fight in you, yet? We string
our fiddles high to keep from their reign.
When manes touch, our pitches are as tight
as cramp, to shiver such songs
from fingers to ear bones. Confess.

Dirce (The Bull's Shadow)

Soon no hands held me but rope did.
Tethered to the bull, our hulls
converged, one resisting the other.
He didn't hold me as much as I held him.
Slapped in the round, I clung
to his flank, to fight the slipping lariat.
Where he carried me, this bronco,
this barrel of meat, where he kicked
his shanks and shook, I cannot tell.
To be under him was his punishment
as much as mine, running to the headache
of bells, their bawling huzzahs.

Bull, you shouldered my weight away,
bowing as you cleft this body
with the hook of your horn. Beast
but not beastly, you looked so wild-eyed
and earnest as you stamped me,
thunderous and gently into the dirt.

Fetlock

Say the Eden was elbowed out by the hill's bones.
      Say she followed his ghost here.

Say any fool can pitch a small blue tent.
      Say not everything is sleeping.

Say they wait for her torch to give out to the night.
      Say the scrape of frogs wakes her.

Say the walls wear the luminous shadows of legs.
      Say they ride roughshod over her.

Say her tent is a trembling bruise on the grass.
      Say this: this is how horses are foaled.

Groundsheet

Before wagons, we slept in sheets
trussed on tension, branches and trust.
Thin as sycamore blades,

our lean-tos harboured the haw-edge,
sheeted-walls tacked with pin thorns.
We add bodies to the anchor

to keep us from chasing the flurry.
From far-flung windows they watched us nest,
called it devil-may-care, marked us Cain.

Here in margins we test our mettle.
We winter with the magpie, kettle our fare
and as St Lawrence's bells ring out

we half-dream, half-ache a stone
under the ground sheet. Know this.
Diamonds are born of pressure.

Aubade

Listen low enough, you'll hear the gennies hum
as a banjo distends a dewy note to the Eden,
eeling North. It was under my footsteps all along,
this hill. Once *Gallows* now called *Fair*, still strung
with our kind and wraithy with ponies who dapple
this dark plot like bulbs newly popped.
My father's father gave this black night to me,
where the sky shifts without permission
as the dawn picks out gilt and bow-top greens,
the chimneys smoke and a nightingale sings.

Passage

Horse by horse,
the street gives another,
until there's a riverful of horses
and then a horseless river.

Caulbearer

When I followed Venus's
wet skirt back into the water,
it wrapped around me
like the caul she bore
my granda in
and breathed:

We of the black curl
bear these tides.
We swallow pearls.
We swallow time.

NOTES AND DEDICATIONS

Inheritance (20): For Granda Jack.

King Faa (21): See David Morley's 'Patrin' in *The Invisible Kings*.

Big Fat Gypsy Swindle (23): According to the Oxford English Dictionary, to gyp or jip is an informal verb of unknown nineteenth-century origin meaning to 'cheat or swindle'. It is alternatively logged as a noun to convey physical discomfort, which the above definitions present the author. The controversial documentary *Big Fat Gypsy Weddings* first aired on Channel 4 in 2010.

Cobsong (24-25): In Romanes, *pétalos* means horseshoe, from the Greek *pétali* for petal or leaf. Appleby Fair is the annual horse market gathering of Travellers in Cumbria.

At Eildon (26): For Damian Le Bas Jnr.

Smithsong (27): For Venus Smith, my Great Grandmother.

Market (28): See Ronan Gallagher's photography of Irish Traveller children for Stella McCartney's *Kids* collection 2017.

The Sly and Unseen Day (30): For my Great Aunt Hazel. A tatter is a rag-and-bone collector, also known as bone grubbers. The title is taken from the 2011 exhibition by George Shaw.

Knots (32): See William Wordsworth's 'Gipsies' (1807).

Larch (33): William Wordsworth's *Guide to the Lakes* (1810) vehemently opposed the introduction of larch plantations. He described the trees, then sprouting by the million and turning 'green long before the native trees' as 'overrunning the hill-sides'. In 'Lines Composed a Few Miles Above Tintern Abbey' (1798) Wordsworth describes the 'wreaths of smoke / Sent up, in silence, from among the trees!'

The Graver (34): See Keats' 'Ode on a Grecian Urn' (1820). 'Whistlejacket' (1762) is a life size oil painting of the titled Arabian horse by George Stubbs.

Outlandish (37): Charlotte Cushman played the character of Meg Merrilies in transatlantic theatrical adaptations of Walter Scott's *Guy Mannering* (1815). Meg is described by Scott as a 'harlot, thief, witch and gipsy'.

Paisley (40): Intricate Kashmiri fabrics were imported from India to the West from the eighteenth century. The popular designs were locally replicated, most notably in Paisley, the Scottish town which gave the pattern its name.

A Stopping-place (42): Benedictine Monk Matthew of Paris (1200-1259) recorded the first irruption of crossbills, in England.

Craft (43): William Morris said in his 1880 lecture: 'have nothing in your house that you do not know to be useful or believe beautiful'. *Shivelight* was coined by Gerard Manley Hopkins in 'That Nature is a Heraclitean Fire and of the comfort of the Resurrection' (1888) to describe how light splinters through trees.

Playing Cards (46): During the Holocaust, black triangles were sewn to Travellers' clothing to identify their 'asocial' status and ethnicity. The Holocaust Memorial Day Trust estimates that in World War Two 200,000 Roma and Sinti Travellers (25% of the population) were killed during the genocide.

Self-portrait as 100 Travellers (48): In 2003 the Firle Bonfire Society, Sussex, paraded an effigy of a caravan bearing the registration plate 'P1KEY' and slogans 'Fair?' and 'As You Likey Driveways'. They then publicly set it alight. A Traveller family with young children were prominently painted on the caravan windows. At the request of the Commission for Racial Equality, the Society apologised for what it said was 'emphatically not a racist comment'.

Nightjar (51): Listen to John Berger and John Christie's *I Send You This Cadmium Red* (1999).

Le Bûcher (53): Italicised lines are taken respectively from the surviving transcript of the 1431 interrogation of Joan of Arc and Gustave Flaubert's 1867 letter to the novelist George Sand.

Periwinkle (55): Twenty-three trafficked Fujian workers died on the night of February 5th 2004 in the Morecambe Bay cockling disaster.

Manes (56): In Roman mythology *manes* are the souls of dead ancestors, worshipped as beneficent spirits. In Newcastle, Haymarket's 'Winged Victory' figure commemorates the men in Northumbrian regiments who lost their lives during the Second Boer War (1899-1902). An estimated 300,000 horses also died in British service.

Rite (59): Appleby Horse Fair in Cumbria is the largest annual gathering of Gypsies, Roma and Travellers in Europe.

Homecoming (62): See *Ars Poetica* by Horace: 'You, that write, either follow tradition, or invent such fables as are congruous to themselves'.

Dirce (The Bull's Shadow) (67): See Thomas Bewick's 'Chillingham Bull' (1789).

Aubade (70): For Dad. See stanza one of Raymond Oliver's translation of Walther von der Vogelweide's medieval lyric 'Under der Linden'.

LIST OF ILLUSTRATIONS

Known as tail-pieces the illustrative vignettes in this collection document bucolic scenes of eighteenth-century North-East England. They were made by Northumberland-born wood engraver Thomas Bewick (1753-1828). Through hand and poster bills these miniature artworks traversed the country as they publicised circuses, menageries and fairs. As letterpress blocks, they were widely used to illustrate books of natural history, broadside ballads and newspapers; were found on packaging wrapped around tobacco and engraved on cutlery; embellished personal bookplates and trade cards; decorated bank notes and family crests; advertised farm stock; adorned invitations to concerts, tickets to balls and event programmes. Bewick's workmanship communicated across classes, counties and areas of commerce, engaged with and drew influence from the worlds of visual art, music and poetry.

As Bewick didn't formally title his engravings, the artworks are here given new titles: